HOW IT HAPPENS
at the ATV Plant

By Jenna Anderson
Photographs by Bob and Diane Wolfe

**CLARA
HOUSE
BOOKS**

Minneapolis

The publisher would like to thank Polaris and its employees for their generous help with this book.

All photographs by Bob and Diane Wolfe except pp. 1, 3, and back cover (courtesy Polaris).

Clara House Books
The Oliver Press, Inc.
Charlotte Square
5707 West 36th Street
Minneapolis, MN 55416-2510

Library of Congress Cataloging-in-Publication Data
Anderson, Jenna, 1977-
    How it happens at the ATV plant / by Jenna Anderson; photographs by Bob and Diane Wolfe.
      p. cm.
    ISBN 1-881508-94-3
    1. All terrain vehicles—Design and construction—Juvenile literature. 2. Assembly-line methods—Juvenile literature. I. Title: At the ATV plant. II. Wolfe, Robert L., ill. III. Wolfe, Diane, ill. IV. Title.

TL278.A53297 2004
629.22'042—dc22

                           2004043909

ISBN 1-881508-94-3
Printed in the United States of America
10 09 08 07 06 05 04   8 7 6 5 4 3 2 1

What if you wanted a vehicle you could use to take a trail ride, mow your lawn, and carry your camping gear? Cars, trucks, and mountain bikes might be able to do some of these things, but an all-terrain vehicle (ATV) can do all three—and more.

Millions of people use these rugged four-wheelers for work and fun every day. ATVs are carefully designed and built to drive off-road, help with yard and farm chores, and transport gear for hunters and campers. This book will give you a behind-the-scenes look at how such multipurpose vehicles are made.

Frame

The first step in building an ATV is making the **frame**—the structure that will support the engine, the wheels, and many other parts. The frame is made of a hard, strong metal called **steel**. Here, a worker puts the different frame pieces in order on a rack.

The pieces are joined together by **welding**—heating and melting them at the spot where they meet. Welding can be hot and sometimes dangerous, so machines called **robots** are programmed to do the work.

Next, the frame and other metal parts are loaded onto racks that will carry them through the painting process. The springs shown here are part of the **shock system**, which makes riding on an ATV less bumpy.

The racks hang on a track that runs throughout the plant. This way, they can be moved easily from place to place.

Paint

The parts are dipped in a liquid that cleans them and gets them ready to be painted. This will help the paint stay on the metal.

The paint needs to be durable because ATVs may be used on rough terrain and in all kinds of weather. The paint is tested many times to make sure it doesn't scratch or chip. The round picture at right shows paint samples that have been scraped with nails and dented to see how the paint holds up.

A worker wearing a protective suit uses a spray gun to coat the parts with paint. The parts will then be moved into a large, hot oven that dries the paint.

METAL PAINT
AND DATA COL

| MONDAY 3RD--1ST--2ND | TUESDAY 3RD--1ST--2ND | WEDNESDAY 3RD--1ST--2ND | 3RD |

WASHER DATA

The painted parts are taken off the rack and sent to the assembly line.

Assembly

The ATV frame hangs on a moving track and travels down an assembly line, where workers add parts to it.

An ATV has four wheels like a car, but it doesn't have a brake pedal. Instead, it has hand brakes, similar to a bicycle or motorcycle. Here, a worker tests the brake lines that will run from the wheels to the handlebars.

The handlebars are also used for steering. When the worker on the right installs them on the ATV frame, she attaches them to the post that directs the wheels.

Then, the wheels and their shock system are attached to the frame. (The tires will be added later.)

The next major item to be added is the **engine**, the part that powers the ATV.

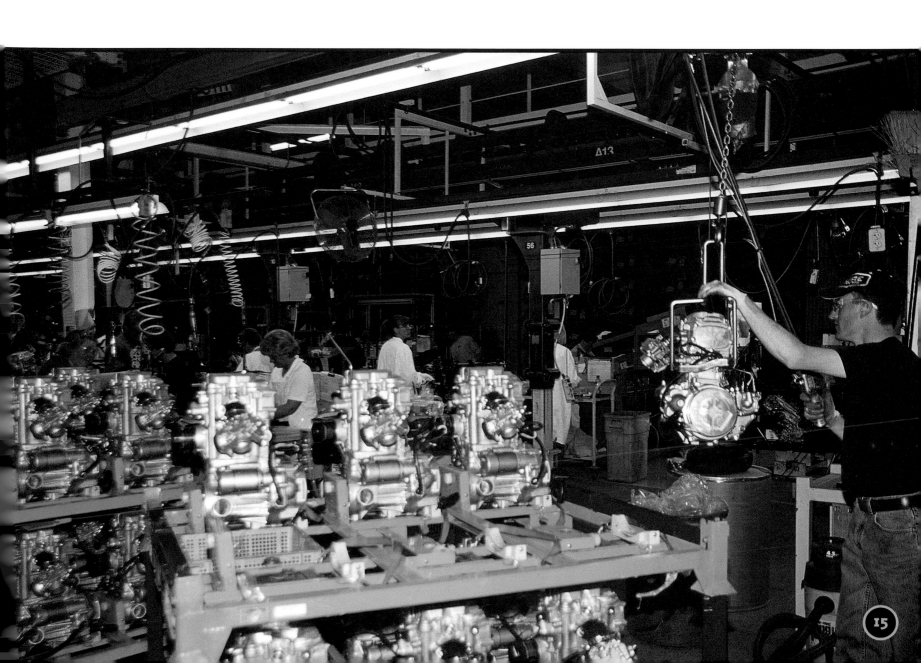

The engine is heavy, so a worker uses a special tool called a **hydraulic lift** to pick it up. Then he can carry it to the frame, where it is installed.

On the assembly line, each worker has a very specific task to do. Many people work on belts, wires, and other small parts that can't be easily seen on the finished vehicle. Even though these pieces are small, they are important. For example, the man in this picture is installing a cable that helps control the ATV's speed.

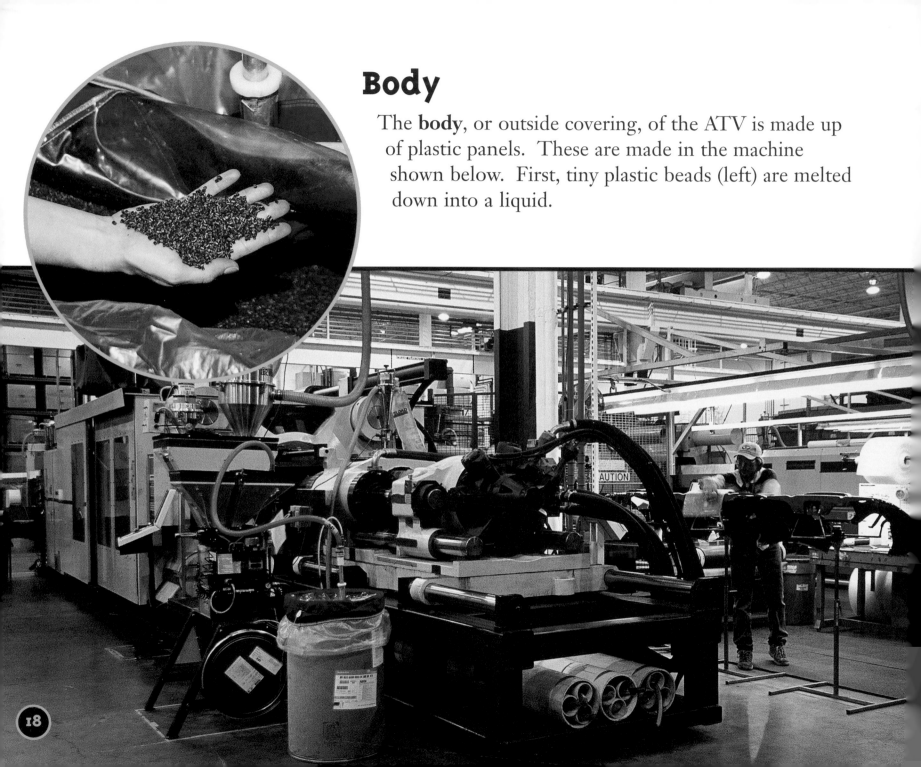

Body

The **body**, or outside covering, of the ATV is made up of plastic panels. These are made in the machine shown below. First, tiny plastic beads (left) are melted down into a liquid.

Then the liquid plastic is injected into a **mold**, a hollow form shaped like one of the ATV body panels. The plastic hardens quickly, taking the shape of the mold.

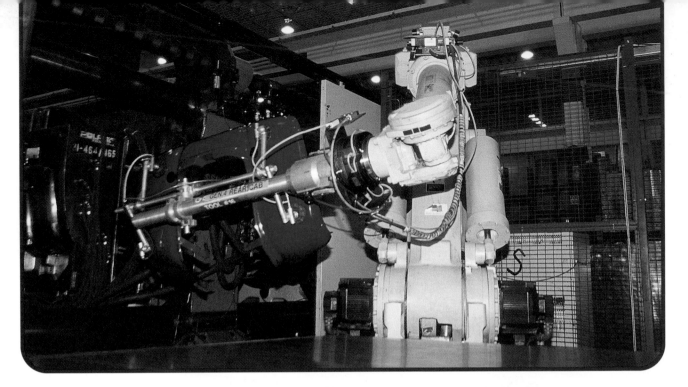

A robot removes the panel from the mold (top left), and an inspector checks to make sure it meets quality standards (bottom left). Then the body pieces are sent over to the assembly line. There, decorative stickers called **decals** are applied to them (above).

The different plastic panels are connected to form the body of the ATV.

Next, the body is placed over the rest of the vehicle.

The last major parts to be added are the tires.

Testing

The finished ATV is put on a **treadmill**, a moving belt that allows the vehicle to be driven while staying in one place. This lets a test driver make sure everything works properly.

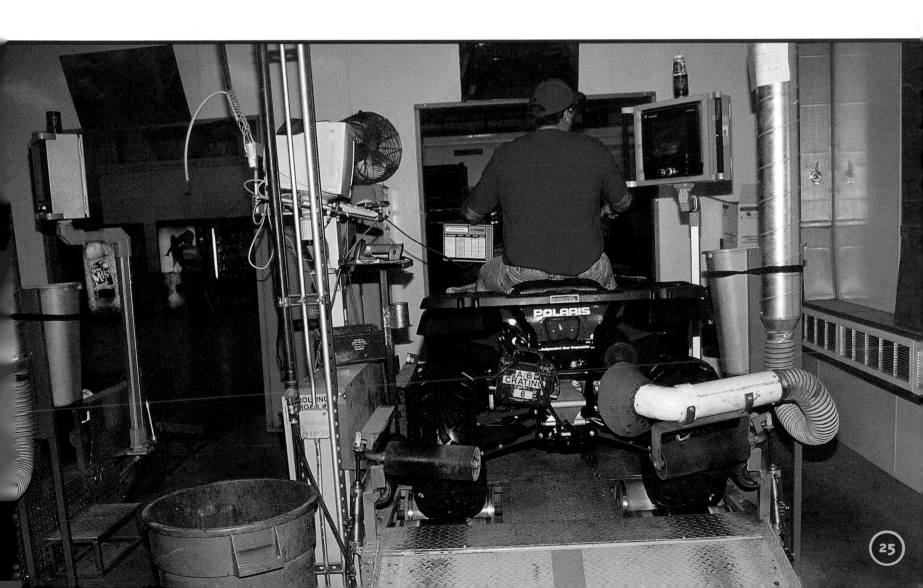

Packaging

A worker drives the ATV up a ramp onto a platform, where an open-sided metal crate is built around it. The crate is a reusable kind of packaging that will protect the vehicle while it is being shipped.

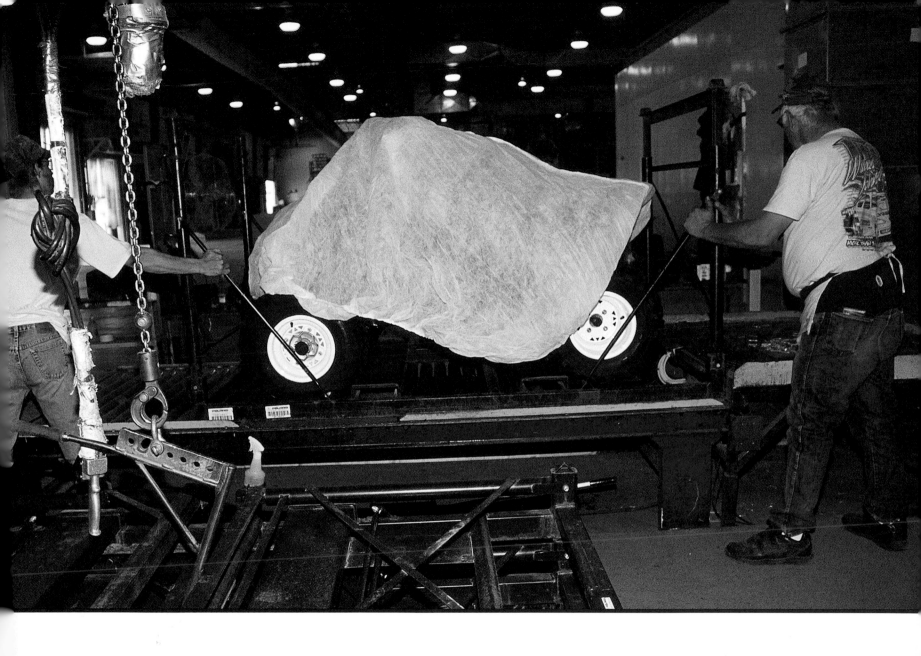

A cover is placed over the ATV to keep it from getting dusty or scratched.

Next, workers enclose the open sides of the crate with a large plastic bag.

A machine **shrink-wraps** the crate by heating the plastic until it fits snugly.

The small size and unique packaging of the ATVs allows the crates to be stacked for shipping. A worker uses a machine called a **forklift** to put the crates on top of one another.

The packaged ATVs are stacked in a shipping yard. They will be loaded onto trucks and sent to dealerships (stores) all over the country. There, they will be sold to people ready to work, play, or just enjoy the great outdoors.

Glossary

body: the outside covering of an ATV, made of plastic panels

decals: decorative stickers

engine: the part that powers the ATV

forklift: a machine that lifts and carries heavy objects from place to place

frame: the steel structure that supports the engine, wheels, and other parts of an ATV

hydraulic lift: a special tool used to pick up and move heavy objects

mold: a hollow form used to shape soft substances

robot: a machine that can be programmed to perform tasks

shock system: a group of parts that make riding on an ATV less bumpy

shrink-wrap: a type of packaging in which plastic is wrapped around a product and heated until it fits snugly

steel: a hard, strong metal

treadmill: a moving belt that allows a vehicle to be driven while staying in one place

welding: a way of joining pieces of metal by heating them at the spot where they meet

Warning:

Polaris ATVs with engine sizes larger than 90cc may not be ridden by anyone under 16 years of age. ATVs with 89cc engines may not be ridden by anyone under 12 years of age. ATVs with 49cc engines may not be driven by anyone under 6 years of age. All riders under 16 should only ride with adult supervision. All riders should take a safety course. For safety and training information, see your dealer or call Polaris at 1-800-342-3764. ATVs can be hazardous to operate. For your safety, always wear a helmet, eye protection and protective clothing. Never ride on public roads; always avoid paved surfaces. Never carry passengers. Never engage in stunt driving. Riding and alcohol/drugs don't mix. Avoid excessive speeds. Be particularly careful on difficult terrain. Remember, ATV riding is more fun when you play by the rules.